Dear reader,

This is a starter book for teaching small children about many of the celebration stories in the Bible. In addition to the weekly Sabbath, there are seven annual "Sabbath" celebrations or holy days that are described in detail in Leviticus 23. Learning about these Bible celebrations gives me even more reasons to celebrate what God has done for me!

The first four celebrations occur in the spring and are especially connected to the Exodus story and Christ's death and resurrection. They are wonderful reminders to us of what God has done to give us a life worth celebrating.

Passover celebrates God's protection and promises. A dramatic rescue story of slavery to freedom is the heritage of the Passover. The release of God's people from slavery in Egypt is the background to the story of Jesus as the Lamb of God who takes away our sins.

Continuing the celebration on the next day, the Festival of Unleavened Bread is named for the seven-day period of time when no food with leaven—a symbol of sin—is eaten. The Festival of Unleavened Bread reminds us of when there was no time for God's people to make bread with leaven because of the preparation to flee Egypt. They ate flatbread in the joy of freedom from slavery. It is also a time to remember Jesus as the Bread of Life and His gift of life through Him.

The Festival of First Fruits celebrates new life. It is a reminder that Noah and his family left the ark and their old life behind and began a new life on this earth. Likewise, after slavery in Egypt, God's people left the water of the Red Sea for a new life. Finally, Jesus came forth from the grave to offer new life as first fruits of the resurrection.

Celebrating God's personal interaction with His people takes place in the Festival of Latter Fruits, which is more commonly known as the Festival of Weeks or Pentecost. Counting fifty days from First Fruits, Latter Fruits celebrates God's closeness at Mount Sinai and how He audibly spoke to His people and gave them the Ten Commandments. Later, God's word made visible when the promised Helper, God's Holy Spirit, fell like tongues of fire on His waiting people. This is a celebration of God becoming a part of His people and His people welcoming Him into their lives.

In the autumn there are three more celebrations! The Bible records these celebrations as part of Jesus' life and mission while on earth. In addition, many believe that while the Bible is not explicit, there is ample evidence that Jesus was born during the Festival of Tabernacles and was also baptized during one of these celebrations. The most exciting aspect of all though is that the autumn celebrations are a special celebration of Christ's second coming.

The Festival of Trumpets is about announcing God's nearness; the blowing of trumpets is said to be for a "memorial" or remembrance. I believe Trumpets is a time to remember what God has done for us in the earlier celebrations. It is a time to proclaim God's authority and goodness in your life. The Festival of Trumpets announces Christ's eminent return.

The Day of Atonement is a celebration of the reconciliation God offers. It is also a somber day of reflection on the sins that separate us from God. Celebrate by settling misunderstandings and hurt feelings with your friends, family, and God and then rejoice in God's love for us! The Day of Atonement is considered the eve of Christ's second coming by many who are watching for Him.

The Festival of Tabernacles celebrates the temporary dwellings of this earth and our permanent home in heaven. Living in tents in the wilderness and Jesus coming to earth to live with us were temporary time periods. The last day of this eight-day celebration is called the Last Great Day. It is the grandest day of the celebration and is filled with food, friends, family, and happiness. It is a sample of heaven and the joy of being with Jesus forever. During the Festival of Tabernacles, we can celebrate that our true home is not of this earth but is waiting for us in heaven, and we can look forward to when we will be with the Jesus forever.

Looking forward to celebrating in heaven together,

Gennifer

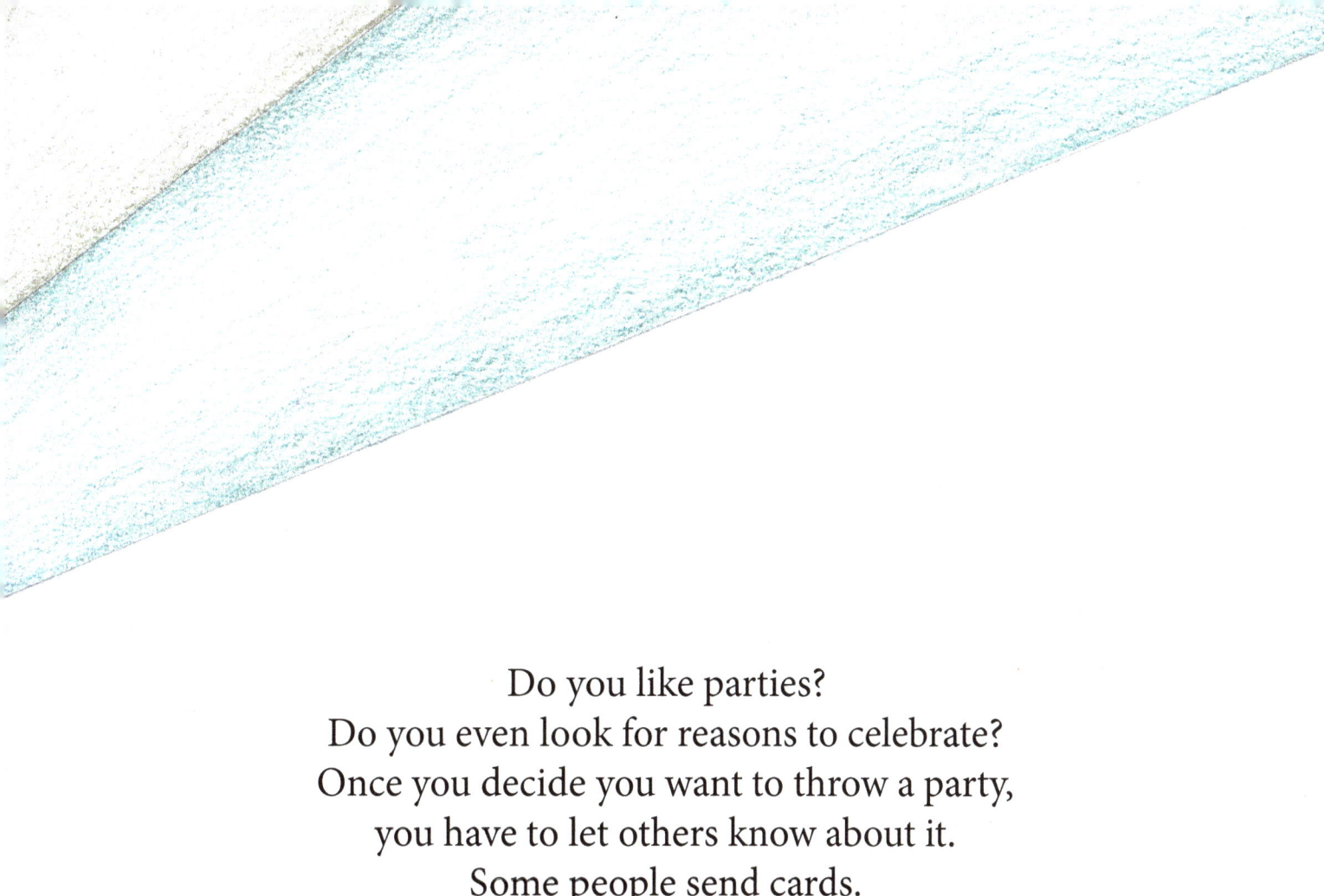

Do you like parties?
Do you even look for reasons to celebrate?
Once you decide you want to throw a party,
you have to let others know about it.
Some people send cards.
Others call on the phone.

Sometimes for really special events, a plane will write across the sky, and then lots of people will see it all at once.

"Wow, that sure is some party over there," they'll say.

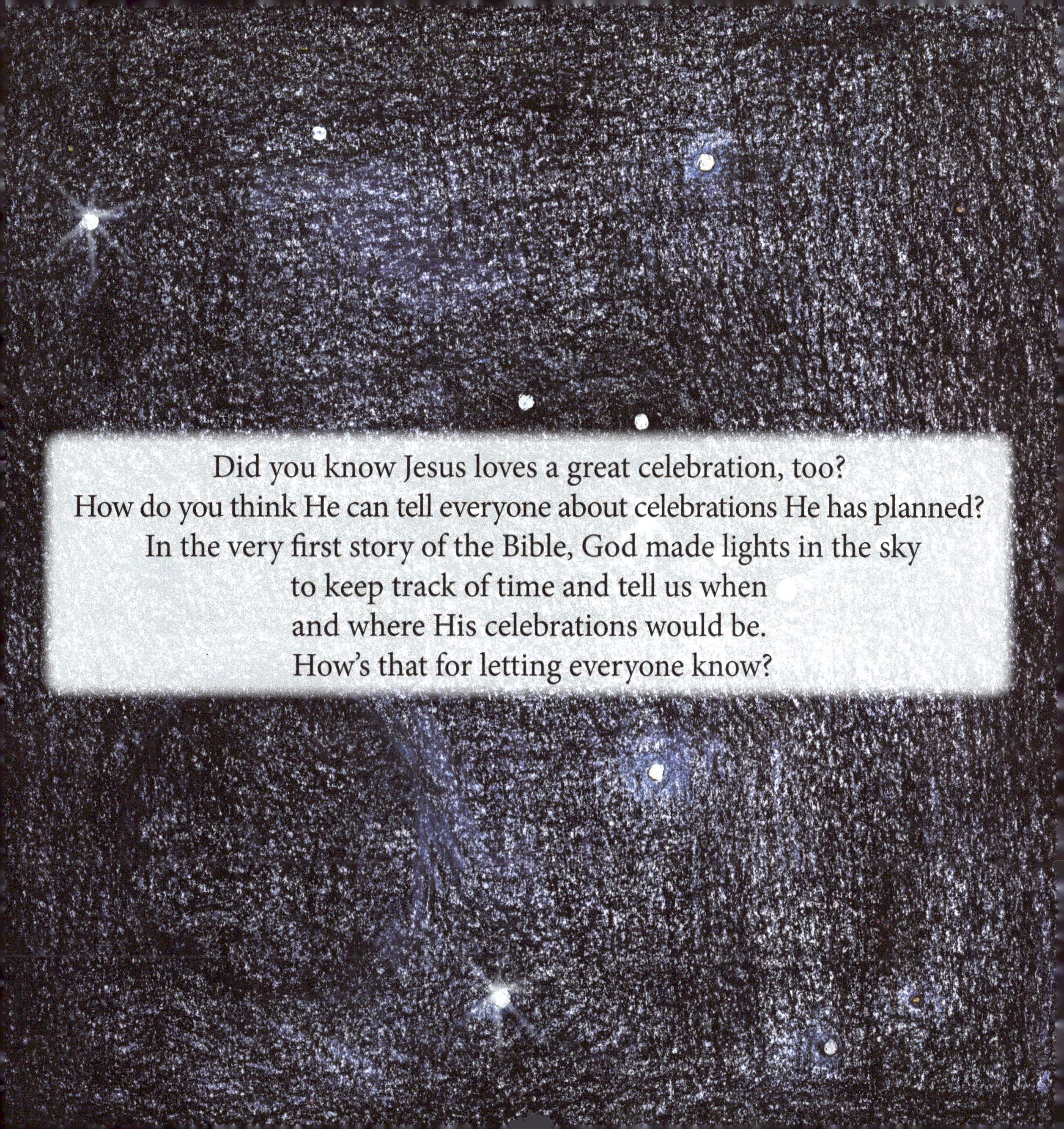

Did you know Jesus loves a great celebration, too?
How do you think He can tell everyone about celebrations He has planned?
In the very first story of the Bible, God made lights in the sky
to keep track of time and tell us when
and where His celebrations would be.
How's that for letting everyone know?

There is an amazing
story in your Bible
about a man named Abraham.
He watched for the celebrations
in the sky and was blessed.

God talked to Abraham and
told him that his children
would move from their
home to Egypt
and become slaves.
But God promised
that they would
be rescued
and come home.

And it happened that way.
Abraham's family lived in Egypt, and they became slaves.
Sadly, they lived there so long they forgot about God's
celebrations. As time went on, conditions grew worse
and even more worse for the slaves! Finally, some people
thought about God and started praying for a rescuer.

God chose Moses as the rescuer. Moses went to Pharaoh and told him, "God says, 'Let my people go. I want them to remember the celebrations I gave them a long time ago with a party celebration planned by Me, and for Me.'"

Pharaoh said "No! I don't know your God,
and I won't listen to Him!"
So God performed many miracles
and allowed many plagues
to fall on the Egyptians so that
Pharaoh would listen and know Him.
But Pharaoh did not want to follow God,
nor did he want to let the people go.

Finally it was time for a celebration!
God told Moses, "Tell the people to get ready to travel."
The Passover's special food was made in a hurry while packing.
There was no time to let the bread finish rising,
so it was baked flat or "unleavened."
This is what they ate while traveling.
Every year from then on the meal for this celebration
especially included flat bread to remind them of being rescued.

It was called the Passover because God "passed over"
their houses and covered the people who asked Him to,
like a parent bird spreads its wings
to protect its babies from an enemy.
This is a happy time—a time to remember
God's protection and promises!

The most important promise of the Passover is about the lamb.
It was to be a perfect, special, beloved lamb,
but it had to die and be prepared in a special way.
This was God's way of reminding His people of Jesus,
His only Son who would come to live in our world
just like that lamb. Jesus was perfect and loved by many,
but He had to die on a Passover to protect and rescue us.
Jesus rescued us from Satan and all the trouble he gives.
In Egypt Pharaoh and many others did not ask for God's
protection and their children died.
Sadly, Pharaoh was only scared; he still did not believe in God.
But he told Moses that the people could leave.
This happened on the exact same day God told
Abraham they would leave more than four hundred years earlier!
What a day to celebrate!

Moses and the people walked for three days until they came
to a big sea. Huge mountains were beside them and behind them, and
the Egyptian army was chasing them from behind!
What was going to happen? How could they celebrate with God?
God made a way to rescues them right through the water.
This day was called the Festival of First Fruits.

Just as you celebrate the first garden produce
that pushes through the dirt and shows new life,
this celebration was the beginning of a new life from Egypt.
When Jesus died as the Passover Lamb, he was buried in a cave.
The Festival of First Fruits was the day
He came out of that burial place to a new life.
We know that just like Jesus who lived again
after He died we, too, can have a new life
when Jesus comes back to take us home.

Mediteranneanean
Sea
HOME
Passover
Pillar of Smoke + fire
Goshen
Nile
Sinai
Wilderness of Zin
Red Sea

For God's people, every step took them
toward their promised home as children of father Abraham.
Every step counted.
Every day counted.
Every day they drew one day closer to their new home.
Each day gave them a chance to get to know God better.
Knowing God better makes us grow
in ways that make home closer.
One, two, three, four, five, six days
and then Sabbath, the seventh day!
Then one, two, three, four, five, six, seven weeks
or forty-nine days passed.

1. Thou shalt have no other gods before me.

2. Thou shalt not make unto thee any graven image.

3. Thou shalt not take the name of the LORD thy God in vain; for the LORD will not hold him guiltless that taketh his name in vain.

4. Remember the Sabbath day, to keep it holy. Six days shalt thou labour, and do all thy work But the seventh day io the Sabbath of the LORD thy God, in it thou shalt not do any work.

5. Honour thy father and thy mother that thy days may be long upon the land which the LORD thy God giveth thee.

6. Thou shalt not kill.

7. Thou shalt not commit adultery.

8. Thou shalt not steal.

9. Thou shalt not bear false witness against thy neighbour.

10. Thou shalt not covet thy neigbour's stuff

The Festival of Latter Fruits takes place
fifty days after the last celebration.
This celebration is about growing up.

During their travels, Moses and the people learned about God
and how to have a new life and grow in Him.
God had a special plan for this celebration.
God Himself would talk directly to the people.

Every person got ready.
They cleaned and scrubbed and cleaned some more.
Then God talked to the people
and gave them the Ten Commandments.
These ten rules were to help the people
grow to be more like God.

When Jesus lived on earth,
the Word of God became a living person.
After Jesus died and rose again,
He promised to send a Helper who could be with all of God's people.

After the Festival of First Fruits and Jesus' resurrection,
He returned to heaven before the fifty days had passed
so that the Holy Spirit could come to the disciples
and His promise of a Helper could come true.

And God's promise came!
It looked like fire, felt like fire,
and spread like fire!
On the first Festival of Pentecost
after Jesus' resurrection,
five thousand people were baptized!
What a celebration for God and all His people!

God's words change people to be more like Jesus,
the Living Word.
It is so wonderful and exciting
that each person just has to share with more people.
What started in Jerusalem has spread
all around the world until millions of people
know about Jesus' special promises.
We always celebrate Pentecost with joy!
It reminds us how God showed us
His great love by giving us His Holy Spirit.

After a long quiet summer, trumpets blow loud for ten days.
It is the celebration called the Festival of Trumpets.
It is a time to remember what God has already done for us.
But trumpets are also for proclaiming things.
It is loud! It is fun!
It is very joyful!
Guess what the Festival of Trumpets is announcing?
Jesus is coming so we can go with Him to heaven!
What a great announcement!
People have been looking for Jesus ever since Pentecost,
and now is a time to tell others about Jesus' soon return!

When we are telling others about Jesus, sometimes they want to know what Jesus looks and acts like. The Day of Atonement (At-One-Ment) is a special celebration to help others know what Jesus looks like and acts like in us! This celebration is different from all the others. It is a quiet day of dressing, eating, and playing simply. Knowing that Jesus is almost here and others are looking at us to see what Jesus looks like sometimes makes us want to be quiet and think about that too. But even though we are quiet, today is an exciting day, too, because Jesus promises that when we want to be like Him, others will see Jesus clearly in us.

After a day of quietness, are you ready
for the biggest celebration ever?
The Festival of Tabernacles is coming up next!
It means "tenting" or, as we would call it, "camping"!
This festival is about us living with
Jesus and Jesus living with us! God's people are to remember
how God had a special tent when
He camped in the wilderness and lived with the Israelites.

The Bible tells us that Jesus "tented" with us when
He came to live here. Jesus was probably even
born during a Tabernacle celebration.
Can you think about a time when
we will all live together with Jesus again?
If you said heaven, you are right!
Tabernacles is about living with Jesus in heaven!
That's really what all of these celebrations are all about—
Jesus loves you and can't wait to celebrate with you in heaven!

Would you like to start celebrating with Jesus now?
The best way to start is by spending time with
Jesus every seventh day on the Sabbath,
which was the very first celebration
in the Bible.

It starts on Friday night, and you can celebrate with candles,
a special supper, and reading stories about Jesus.
Sabbath is a great day to do something at church,
be outside, or spend time with friends.
It is also the time to celebrate your friendship with Jesus
and His love for you! What could be better than spending an
entire day each week with Jesus? The Bible celebrations help us
remember who Jesus is and what He has done for us.
Sabbath is our weekly celebration with our Savior!

We invite you to view the complete
selection of titles we publish at:

www.TEACHServices.com

Scan with your mobile
device to go directly
to our website.

Please write or email us your praises, reactions, or
thoughts about this or any other book we publish at:

P.O. Box 954
Ringgold, GA 30736

info@TEACHServices.com

TEACH Services, Inc., titles may be purchased in bulk for
educational, business, fund-raising, or sales promotional use.
For information, please e-mail:

BulkSales@TEACHServices.com

Finally, if you are interested in seeing
your own book in print, please contact us at

publishing@TEACHServices.com

We would be happy to review your manuscript for free.

www.ingramcontent.com/pod-product-compliance
Lightning Source LLC
Chambersburg PA
CBHW042024180426
43200CB00034B/2993